Guitar *QuickStart*

A Guide to Playing and Understanding

Music Reading

and

Chord Techniques

by Mary Jo Disler

Lyra House

ISBN: 0-9642229-0-6

Lyra House Music Publications
P.O. Box 252132, West Bloomfield, MI 48325-2132
(248) 855-2135, phone or fax
Email: Lyrahpub@aol.com

Website: iteachguitar.com

llustrations by Patricia M. O'Connor.
Cover art by Madeline Dupuie
Cover graphic design by B. J. Graphics, Ypsilanti, Michigan

Printed in the United States of America.

10 9 8 7 6 5 4 3 2

◗ Contents

◗ Introduction

Guitar QuickStart is an entry-level book. It is the result of over twenty years of teaching
guitar: both privately and in classes for beginners at college level. Both note-reading and chord
/ rhythm playing are presented. The approach is straight-ahead practicality for students anxious
to play the instrument. There is nothing quite so practical, however, as establishing a thought
process – or theory – which will enable one to access material beyond the basics. That is the
intent of this book. Direction in "how to play" is accompanied by information and workbook
material relating the guitar to music theory. Following *QuickStart,* students may continue with
one of the many excellent methods for either classic or steel-string guitar.

The guitar is a wonderful learning experience because it is accessible through both graphics and
music staff notation. Each system communicates something that the other cannot. Working
together, they provide insight into skill, technique and musical logic. The string-and-fretboard
grid of the guitar permits a graphic reference known as "tablature." Tablature has an important
historic role in guitar music, especially prior to 1750. In the late eighteenth century, however,
experiments modelled on writing for violin eventually led to the adoption of staff notation as the
standard for classic guitar music. Any serious student of guitar today *must* learn to read music.

Guitar QuickStart is a unique modern text because it uses a simplified version of tablature for
the express purpose of relating music staff notation to the fretboard. Tablature is having a
modern day revival in many publications for guitar. Most of these books, however, use it as a
substitute for learning to read. In *QuickStart,* tablature is *not* used as a crutch to avoid true
music reading: Rather, it is intended to be a temporary tool for helping new music readers
visualize the relationship between the fretboard and notation.

Guitar QuickStart is an excellent resource for classes in beginning guitar. Most of this book can
be taught in a one semester course of two credit hours. Many aspiring guitarists are
experiencing music study for the first time. Learning to read rhythmic notation can be especially
vexing for beginners. A valuable by-product of learning music from guitar is that chord work
provides the opportunity to read rhythmic notation independently. – And rhythms are
associated with physical motion through strumming patterns. In addition, the association of
music notation to fretboard through tablature is a very practical testing device for teachers.

Guitar QuickStart can be self-studied to great advantage. There is, however, no real substitute
for working with a good teacher. The subtleties of technique and sound simply cannot be
conveyed through any book. – Nor can the special needs and talents of an individual be
adequately met.

It is the author's sincere wish that you will have fun with ***Guitar QuickStart*** and that it will be
of genuine value in working toward your goals on the guitar.

To Karl,
Erik, and Edith

"The trees of the wood sing out for joy before the Lord"   – I Chronicles 16:33

▶ *Chapter 1*

The Guitar

▶ A. Types of Guitar

Because they are essentially handmade, it is relatively easy for guitar makers to experiment with design, and there are countless versions of guitars available today. Nevertheless there are four basic designs in today's instruments: classic, acoustic steel string, ƒ-hole hollow-body, and solid body electric.

1. *Classic Guitar.*

On the classic guitar the neck and body meet at the twelfth fret. It uses nylon strings. Three strings are true nylon, and three are metal-wound. The tension of the strings is far less than that of steel strings, so there is no support rod in the neck. *Never put steel strings on a guitar made for nylon. The neck may eventually warp or break beyond repair.*

This is the guitar generally recommended for beginners. The lighter string tension and the wider neck make it easier to handle during the early stages of building strength in the left hand. It is played with fingers rather than a pick, and is an excellent all-purpose guitar, suitable to classic, folk, and jazz.

2. *Solid Body Electric Guitar.*

[not pictured]

The solid body electric guitar is used mainly by rock guitarists. The action [distance of the strings from the fretboard] makes it much easier for the fretting hand. Although it is usually played with a pick, some players use it for very sophisticated finger-style playing.

3. Acoustic Steel String Guitar.

The term "acoustic" properly applies to *any* guitar which is not dependent on electronic amplification. On the acoustic steel string guitar the neck and body meet at the fourteenth fret. It uses steel strings with very high tension, so there is a support rod in the neck. This rod can be adjusted by a qualified repair person if the neck should warp over time. Nylon strings can be used on a guitar made for steel strings without causing structural damage, but the sound is generally inferior, and the low action may cause nylon strings to buzz on the frets.

The narrower neck and high string tension may be difficult for beginners. It is played with either pick [plectrum] or fingers,

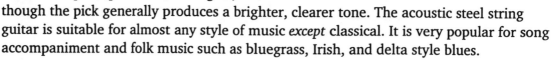

though the pick generally produces a brighter, clearer tone. The acoustic steel string guitar is suitable for almost any style of music *except* classical. It is very popular for song accompaniment and folk music such as bluegrass, Irish, and delta style blues.

The **twelve-string guitar** groups the strings into six sets of two (six "courses"). In the lower four sets, a low string is paired with one which sounds an octave higher. In the higher two sets, the two strings are at the same pitch level [in "unison"]. Chord forms and playing techniques are generally the same as for the acoustic steel string guitar, though finger style playing is hampered by the close spacing between the string sets. Tuning and fingering are usually difficult for beginners. One string in each pair may be removed temporarily if desired.(If so, the "thinner," higher sounding string should be the one removed from the lower four pairs.)

4. ƒ-hole Hollow-body Guitar.

The ƒ-hole hollow-body guitar has scroll-shaped sound holes, similar to those of the orchestral strings, on either side of the bridge. Older instruments are entirely acoustic, but modern versions usually have pickups. It is generally played at low levels of amplification and has a more mellow sound than the solid-body electric. The ƒ-hole guitar is enjoying a renewal of interest, and is often preferred by jazz guitarists.

◗ B. Posture and Position for Holding the Guitar.

1. *Classic Guitar.*

• Sit forward on the chair so the guitar is in front of the seat, not on your lap.
• Place the left foot on the footstool.
• Place the left knee directly in line with the center of your face.
• Establish an axis lining up the spine – nose – knee – music.
• Posture should be straight, balanced, not tense. Do not crouch over the guitar.
• Place the "waist" of the guitar over the left knee.
• Rest the right elbow *on top* of the guitar's side edge, *never in front.*
• Let the right hand hang across the strings at a right angle.
• The end of the fretboard should be approximately shoulder high.
• The left arm should hang loosely from the shoulder, free to flow with the left hand .
• Generally, the left elbow will be close to the body. Avoid "winging" it out.
• Use the right elbow to push the guitar body to a comfortable position.
• *Bring the guitar to you!* Don't bend your back to follow it around.

2. *Acoustic Steel String Guitar.*

Follow the directions for the classic guitar, with the following exceptions:
• Place the *right* foot on the footstool, if height is needed for stability.
• Place the "waist" of the guitar over the *right* knee.

◗ C. Hand and Guitar Symbols.

1. *Circled Numbers are used for strings.*
In this diagram, the vertical lines are strings and the horizontal lines are frets. Strings have both numbers and letter names. The term "open strings" refers to strings as tuned, with no fingered frets. The sixth string ⑥ is the thickest, lowest sounding one. The first string ① is the thinnest, highest sounding string.

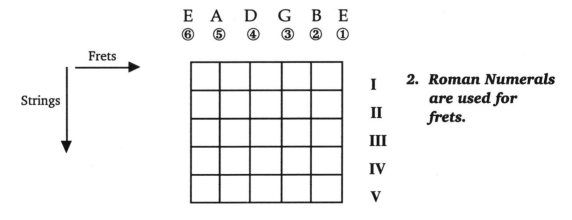

2. *Roman Numerals are used for frets.*

3. Left hand fingers *are labelled with arabic numerals.*	**1**	index finger
	2	middle finger
The thumb is behind the neck, and is not given a number.	**3**	ring finger
	4	little finger

4. Right hand fingers *are labelled with letters from Spanish words for the fingers.*	**P**	Thumb
	I	Index finger
	M	Middle finger
The little finger is used for strumming, but almost never for plucking a single string. It is not given a letter.	**A**	Ring finger

▶D. Playing Techniques for Single Strings.

1. *Pick.* The pick is recommended for steel strings. Use downstrokes on each string with the pick ("plectrum"), letting it fall lightly onto the next string. This stops the pick and helps to relax the hand. It also controls the number of strings played when reading notes which are on inner strings.

2. *Fingers.* Fingers are recommended for playing nylon strings. As a beginning technique, use the index ("*i*") and middle ("*m*") fingers of the right hand.
   • Pull the string gently but firmly inward, and bump lightly into the next string after each stroke, thus "resting" on it briefly. This is called a "reststroke," or *apoyando* in classical guitar terminology.
   • Alternate the index and middle fingers, as though they were "walking."
   • The thumb ("*p*") may be used, but should be limited to strings ⑥ , ⑤ , and ④ until your technique is further developed. Avoid the tendency to play everything with the thumb. The thumb should play a reststroke: push the string gently but firmly downward, and bump lightly into the next string.
   • Finger technique is possible on steel-string guitars, but is complicated somewhat by holding the guitar on the right knee. Experiment to see if it will work for you.

   • *Play and memorize the open string numbers and letter names.*

▶ E. "High" and "Low" in Musical Sound.

The terms "high" and "low" describe the relationships of musical tones. It is important to relate sound to the graphic representations of the fretboard, because they are not always parallel. For example, string ① is the *highest sounding* string, but it is positioned as the *lowest* string when holding the guitar. Study the following diagram to clarify the relationships of "high and low" pitch in sound and on the fretboard.

Low   *High*

Lower frequency sound waves   Higher frequency sound waves

Male voices   Female voices

Left area of piano keyboard   Right area of piano keyboard

Left area of the guitar fretboard   Right area of the guitar fretboard

Thicker strings of the guitar   Thinner strings of the guitar

E A D G B E
⑥ ⑤ ④ ③ ② ①

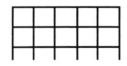

When playing open strings on the guitar from "thinner to thicker," the sound *gets lower.*	When playing open strings on the guitar from "thicker to thinner," the sound *gets higher.*
On a single string, the lower numbered frets are lower in sound. The longer the string, the lower the sound.	On a single string, the higher numbered frets are higher in sound. The shorter the string, the higher the sound.
In playing single frets *toward the left*, the sound *gets lower.*	In playing single frets *toward the right*, the sound *gets higher.*
To *lower* a tone [pitch] when tuning, *loosen* the string. If a note is "too high" it must be *lowered by loosening* the string.	To *raise* a tone [pitch] when tuning, *tighten* the string. If a note is "too low" it must be made *higher by tightening* the string.

Chart © Mary Jo Disler, 1986

[This page is blank to permit the best page turns later in the book.]

▶ F. Parts of the Guitar.

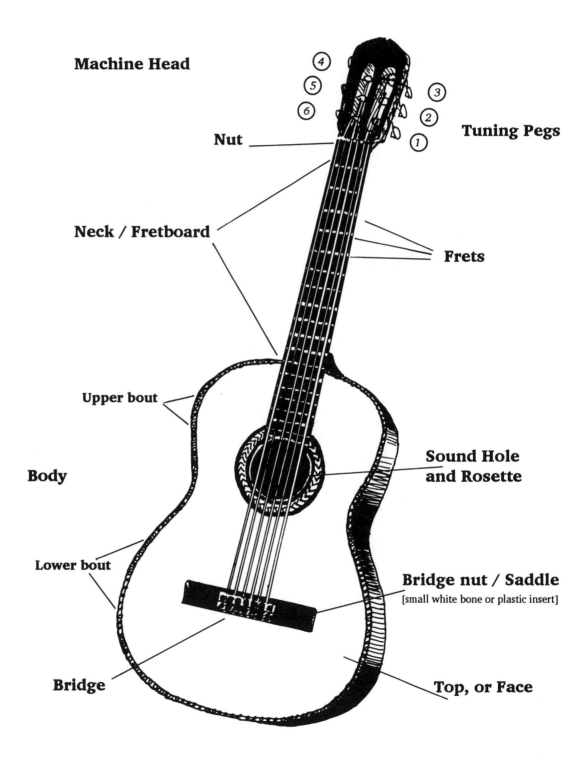

Machine Head

④ ⑤ ⑥

③ ② ①

Nut

Tuning Pegs

Neck / Fretboard

Frets

Upper bout

Body

Sound Hole
and Rosette

Lower bout

Bridge nut / Saddle
[small white bone or plastic insert]

Bridge

Top, or Face

▶ *Chapter 2*

The Guitar Fretboard

▶ A. Music Theory and the Fretboard: Whole- and Half-steps.

An overview of the entire guitar fretboard is helpful as background for learning specific areas. To provide this overview, a formula of whole- and half-steps will be used to locate the alphabet letters used in music on each string. The terms "whole-step" and "half-step" may be applied to music on any instrument, and provide a link to working with other musicians and to learning the basic formulas of music in the western cultural tradition. In its broad outlines, the study of these formulas is called "music theory."

1. A half-step is a distance of one fret on the same string.

Examples of half-steps are shown on these fretboard diagrams:

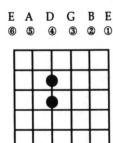 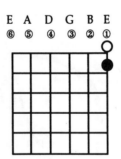 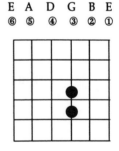

• *In the chart below, write the fret numbers a half-step higher and lower from the given fret number*:*

Fret Number	Fret Half-step Higher	Fret Half-step Lower
A. II	_____	_____
B. VII	_____	_____
C. IV	_____	_____
D. Open string	_____	_____
E. I	_____	_____

*Answers for most workbook material are provided in "Reference C," pp.81 – 85.

• On the diagrams below, mark the frets a half-step higher or lower as indicated:

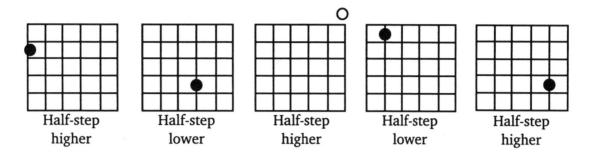

| Half-step higher | Half-step lower | Half-step higher | Half-step lower | Half-step higher |

2. A whole-step is a distance of two frets on the same string.

Examples of whole-steps are shown on these fretboard diagrams:

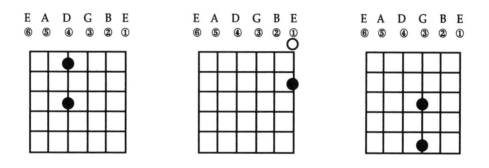

• On the chart below, write the fret numbers a whole-step higher and lower from the given fret number:

Fret Number	Fret Whole-step Higher	Fret Whole-step Lower
A. III	_____	_____
B. IX	_____	_____
C. II	_____	_____
D. Open string	_____	_____
E. I	_____	_____

• On the diagrams below, mark the frets a whole-step higher or lower as indicated:

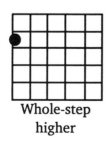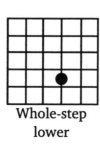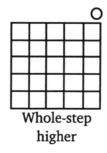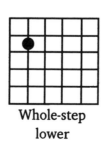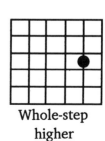

| Whole-step higher | Whole-step lower | Whole-step higher | Whole-step lower | Whole-step higher |

9

▶ B. Alphabet Letters Used in Music Theory.

Music uses the alphabet letters A through G. Unaltered alphabet letters (those with no sharps or flats) are termed "natural notes."

- Letters are in *alphabetical order* when pitches (tones) get consecutively *higher*

$$\text{A} \quad \text{B} \quad \text{C} \quad \text{D} \quad \text{E} \quad \text{F} \quad \text{G} \quad \text{A}$$

- Letters are in *reverse order* when pitches get consecutively *lower.*

> **Most natural notes are a whole-step apart**
> *except B to C and E to F,*
> *which are a half-step apart.*

- *To test your understanding of this important rule, complete the following statement by filling in the blanks:*

Most natural notes are _____ [number] fret(s) apart,

except B to C and E to F,

which are _____ [number] fret(s) apart.

Examples of whole- and half-steps are shown on these fretboard diagrams:

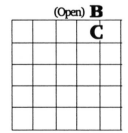

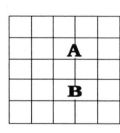

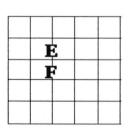

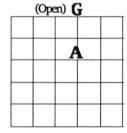

B – C is a half-step: one fret.	A – B is a whole-step: two frets.	E – F is a half-step: one fret.	G – A is a whole-step: two frets.

10

In the following chart, mark the appropriate answers. (Item "a" is marked as an example.)

	Letters	Half-step	Whole-step	One fret	Two frets
a.	**F – G**		✓		✓
b.	**C – D**				
c.	**B – C**				
d.	**D – E**				
e.	**A – B**				
f.	**E – F**				
g.	**G – A**				

On the following fretboards single letters are marked and named.

- *Use a dot to mark the new note [letter] on the same string, according to the directions.*
- *Write the letter name of the new note in the blank provided.*

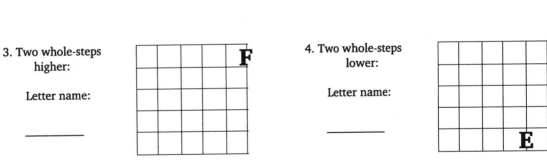

1. Whole-step higher:

   Letter name:

   _____

2. Whole-step lower:

   Letter name:

   _____

3. Two whole-steps higher:

   Letter name:

   _____

4. Two whole-steps lower:

   Letter name:

   _____

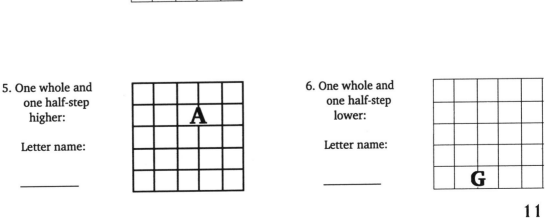

5. One whole and one half-step higher:

   Letter name:

   _____

6. One whole and one half-step lower:

   Letter name:

   _____

▶ C. Letters on the Entire Fretboard to Fret Twelve.

The whole- and half-step patterns may be used as a formula to locate letter names anywhere on the fretboard. The open-string name provides the starting letter. The frets skipped for whole-steps serve as sharps or flats for the letters on either side. DO NOT diagram these frets here. Focus on learning the "plain letters" [naturals] first.

• *Using the whole- and half-step patterns, mark the locations of all letters [natural notes]*
from the open string to fret twelve [XII] on each string of the tablature below.
String ⑥ is done as an example.

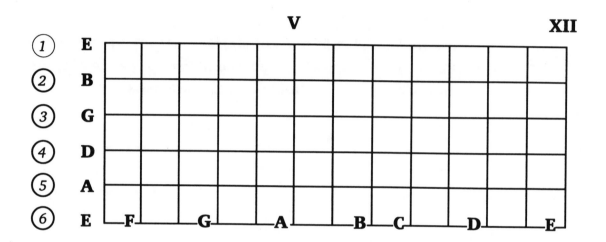

After all the letters are marked on the fretboard above, answer these questions:

1. What is the number of the fret that has the same letter names as the open strings? Fret number _____ .

    • ***This fret is one octave higher than the same string played "open."***

2. Very few frets have letters [natural notes] across all six strings. Which frets are they? _____ .

3. Which frets have letters on all but one string? _____

4. Only one fret has *no* natural letters on any string. Which fret? _____

5. Which frets have only *one* letter on any of the strings? _____

   • *Play the alphabet on each string, from the open string to fret XII and back.*
   • *Place the second [middle] finger of the left hand just to the left of the fret, with the thumb directly opposite, behind the neck of the guitar. The thumb should be across the neck, as though it were a "fret."*
   • *Slide the second finger to each letter and play it twice with pick or reststroke "i-m."*

▶ D. Building a Scale of Natural Notes in First Position.

In section C of this chapter, an alphabet has been constructed horizontally on the guitar fretboard, from each open string letter to fret twelve of the same string. The guitar is multi-dimensional. It is also possible to build an alphabet by *changing strings* in the same area, or "position," on the fretboard.

1. *Positions on the guitar are numbered by the fret where the first finger of the left hand is located.*

    For example, when the first finger is at fret I, the hand is in "first position." The fingers line up at frets I, II, III and IV. If the first finger is at fret V, and the other fingers line up at frets VI, VII, and VIII, the hand is in "fifth position."

2. *A scale can be constructed in first position [open string through fret IV] by filling in the letters missing between the open strings.*

    Shown here are the open strings in order from the lowest to the highest sounding:

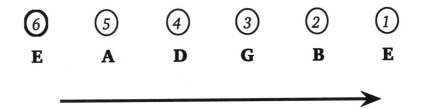

    As the open strings are played in the above order, the sound gets *higher*. When the sound gets higher, the alphabet is *in order*. Therefore the missing letters between the open strings may be filled in by simply completing the alphabet.

    • *Fill in a complete alphabet below. It has been started for you.*

    E $\mathcal{F}$ $\mathcal{G}$ A __ __ D __ __ G__ B __ __ E __ __

This order of letters is a scale of natural notes as played *across* the strings in first position. The given letters are played as open strings, and the filled-in letters are fretted with the left hand, as in this example. Notice that the whole- and half-steps determine the frets used, just as they did for the horizontal scale to fret XII.

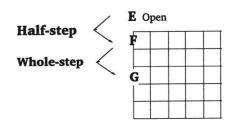

• *Fill in the missing information in this chart. The sixth string is done as a sample.*

Open Strings:	E		A			D			G			B		E		
Fretted Tones:	*F*	*G*	_	_	_	_	_	_	_	_	_	_	_	_	_	_
Whole- or Half-steps (**W** or **H**) :	*H*	*W*	_	_	_	_	_	_	_	_	_	_	_	_	_	_
Fret Numbers:	*O*	*I*	*III*	_	_	_	_	_	_	_	_	_	_	_	_	_

• *Finish marking the letters of the first position scale on this tablature. It has been started as an example. Be sure to write the scale for first position only, NOT for the entire fretboard. The higher part of the fretboard [the right area] should be blank when you are finished. The purpose of this exercise is to orient you to finding the scale in one position only.*

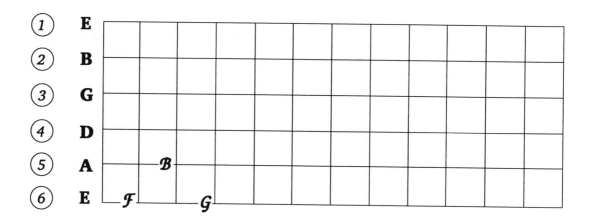

3. *Play the scale in alphabetical order, and reversed: ascending and descending.*

   A. **Play each letter twice**: either down-up with a pick, or "i m" with fingers using a reststroke.

   B. **Play each letter once.** Use all down-strokes with a pick, or "i m" with fingers using a reststroke.

▶ Chapter 3

Reading Music on the Guitar

▶ A. The Music Staff.

Music is notated on a staff of five lines, using both lines and spaces. The staff is like a graph of the sounds produced.

1. Notes placed higher on the lines and spaces sound successively higher when played.

2. Notes placed lower on the lines and spaces sound successively lower when played.

3. Notes successively higher on the staff are alphabetically in order.

   • *Finish writing the letter names below each note on this staff:*

G   A   B _____

4. *Notes successively lower on the staff are alphabetically reversed.*

  • *Finish writing the letter names below each note on this staff:*

G F E _____

5. *Whole- and half-steps are not visible on the staff. Only the alphabetical order is shown.*

▶ B. Relating the Music Staff to Letters on the Fretboard.

Because the line/space levels of the staff are alphabetically successive, the letter names for an entire staff can be established by naming just one of those levels.

1. *The letter "G" is located on the guitar staff by the G-clef sign, which derives from the actual letter "G."*

It names the second line from the bottom of the staff "G". Any note with this line through its center (referred to as G "on the second line") is named "G."

2. *The clef-sign G represents just one of the G's in the first position scale.*

  • *Review the letter names of the natural notes in first position by writing them below, then answer the questions following on the next page.*

String: ⑥ ____⌐ ⑤ ____⌐ ④ ____⌐ ③ __⌐ ② ____⌐ ① ____⌐

Letter: _E_ _F_ __ __ __ __ __ __ __ __ __ __ __ __ __ __ __

Questions:

How many times does the letter "G" occur in this scale? _____.

The *low* G is on string number _____, fret number _____.

The *middle* G is on string number _____, fret number _____.

The *high* G is on string number _____, fret number _____.

The "G" shown by the G-clef represents the *Middle G* *played on string ③ open.*

❱ C. Basic Rhythm Reading.

Location of notes on the lines and spaces indicate letter names. The *length of time* notes are to sound is shown by notation of rhythm. To learn the counting values of the commonly used notes: quarter note, half-note, dotted half-note and whole note, play and count these examples. As a beginning technique for counting, say the number of beats for each note individually, as described. [The vertical lines group notes into "measures." Each measure has the same total number of beats.]

1. *The quarter note is a black note with a stem.*
   Count 1 beat for each. (Say "1" for each)

2. *The half note is a white note with a stem.*
   Count 2 beats for each. (Say "1 – 2" for each)

3. **The dotted half note is a white note with a stem and dot.**
Count 3 beats for each. (Say "1 – 2 – 3" for each)

4. **The whole note is a white note with no stem.**
Count 4 beats for each. (Say "1 – 2 – 3 – 4" for each)

5. **A time signature is the set of 2 numbers at the beginning of a piece.**
The top number is the total number of beats in each measure. The number underneath is symbolic of the kind of note that gets one beat. Most often the bottom number is "4," representing the quarter note. The letter "**C**" is the same as the time signature 4/4.

▶ D. First Position Reading Charts and Exercises.

Alphabet letters provide the link connecting staff notation to the fretboard. A brief survey of the letters and notation on all of the strings in first position is provided here. Study and play these short introductory exercises for each string separately. If you have never read music before, it is like learning a new language. Program the information as you play.

> • **Your own voice is your own best teacher.**
>
> • **Speak aloud one of the following as you play:**

Note names.   • *Say "E, F, G," etc.*

Fret numbers.   • *Say "open, I, III," etc.*

Counting numbers. • *Say "1, 1 – 2, 1 – 2 – 3," etc.*

➤   **After completing this chapter**, and the following chapter which relates notation to extended tablature, choose a reading method book suitable to your goals and technique (plectrum or classic "finger" technique.)

1. *Third String.*

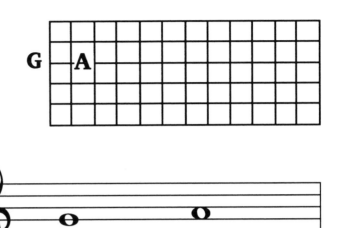

String ③   **G**   **A**

Fret number: O   II

Exercise #1

Exercise #2

Write your own exercise using "G" and "A."

2. Second String.

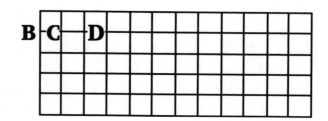

String ②   **B**   **C**   **D**

Fret number: O   I   III

Exercise #3

Write your own exercise using "B," "C," and "D."

3. First String.

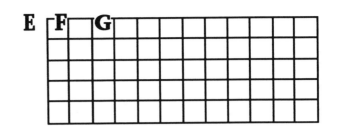

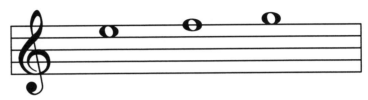

String ①   **E**   **F**   **G**

Fret number: O   I   III

Exercise #4

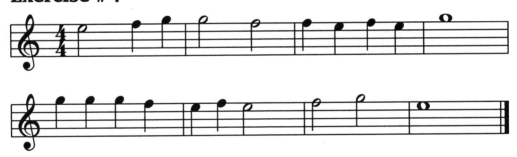

Write your own exercise using high "E," "F," and "G."

4. Sixth String.

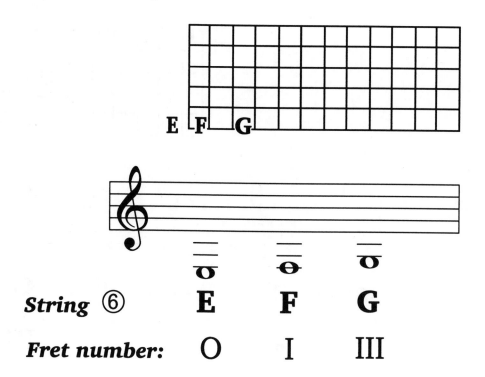

String ⑥   **E**   **F**   **G**

Fret number: O   I   III

Exercise #5

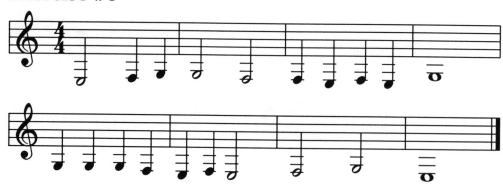

Write your own exercise using low "E," "F," and "G."

5. *Fifth String.*

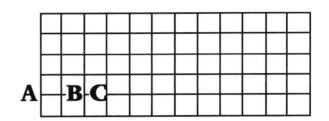

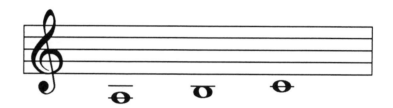

String ⑤   **A**   **B**   **C**

Fret number: O   II   III

Exercise #6

Write your own exercise using "A," "B," and "C."

6. *Fourth String.*

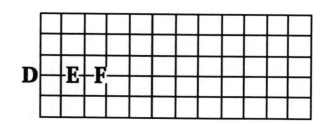

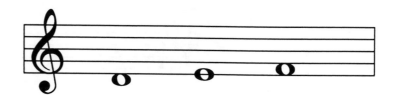

String ④   **D**   **E**   **F**

Fret number: O   II   III

Exercise #7

Write your own exercise using "D," "E," and "F."

First Position Natural Scale

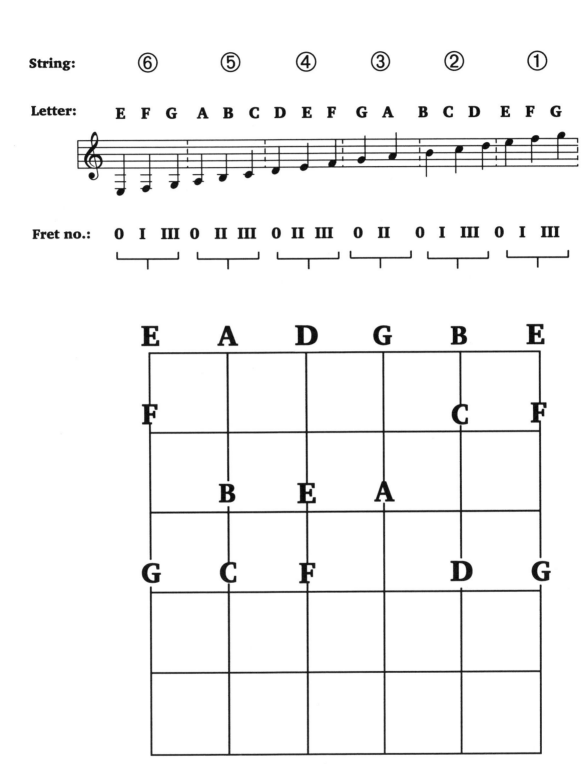

▶ *Chapter 4*
Guitar Tablature and Notation

▶ A. Pitch Levels of Letters and the Music Staff.

In music theory, the term "pitch class" designates all notes with the same letter name (including sharps or flats). Alphabet letters are the link between fretboard and music staff, but it is also important to distinguish the correct *pitch level.* For example, the pitch class "E" occurs at three levels in the first position scale: *low E* (string ⑥ open), *middle E* (string ④ fret II), and *high E* (string ① open). The Low E *sounds* the lowest of the three. The High E *sounds* the highest, and the Middle E sounds at a level between these two. Therefore they are shown at low, middle, and high levels on the music staff.

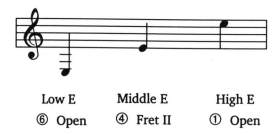

Low E	Middle E	High E
⑥ Open	④ Fret II	① Open

• *When reading in first position, keep this principle in mind:*

> **Notes that are *higher* on the staff
> are on *higher* strings.**
>
> **Notes that are *lower* on the staff
> are on *lower* strings.**

➤ **Special information:** Guitar pitch is *one octave lower* than if the same notes were played on the piano, or at "concert pitch." Some guitar publications show this octave difference by a G-clef sign with an "8" underneath.

• *Note placement on strings and frets is the same for both types of G-clef sign: with or without the "8."*

▶ B. Converting Music Notation to Guitar Tablature.

It is helpful to visualize the place of each note on the fretboard in the order it is played. Over time the reading process can be transformed into a kind of choreography which mentally plans the pathway of the fingers. The fretboard becomes a stage upon which the fingers, hand and arm trace patterns of movement resulting from the order and configurations of notes.

As a step in creating a "mental choreography," notation can be converted to written tablature. Tablature is a "picture" of the fretboard at a moment in time. Six lines representing the guitar strings are shown beneath the music staff. The *highest* line represents the *highest* sounding string, ① . The *lowest* line represents the *lowest* sounding string, ⑥ .

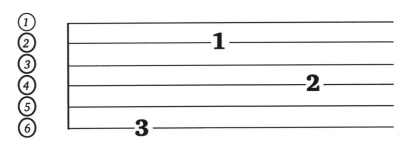

The fretboard location for a note on the music staff may be shown by writing the fret number on the corresponding string. The example above shows fret 3 on string ⑥ , fret 1 on string ② , and fret 2 on string ④ .

The tablature exercises in this book are a helpful introduction for associating notation with the fretboard. As your note-reading experience develops, however, you will not find it necessary to make the conversion to tablature. The goal is to read directly from staff notation to the guitar.

• *1. For the "Ode to Joy" on the next page, mark the tablature lines directly below each note with the correct fret number, or "o" for "open," on the correct string. Use arabic numerals. After writing the tablature, play the piece.*

Ode to Joy

From the Ninth Symphony

Ludwig van Beethoven

The "Ode to Joy" has some notes for which the counting has not yet been explained. Since this piece is probably familiar, play the rhythms "by ear" as you are used to hearing them.

• In measures 4, 8 and 16, the dotted quarter & 8th notes have a "long - short" effect.

1 2 &

• In measures 10 and 11, the *two eighth-notes* connected by a beam are equal to the time of *one quarter note*. They occur on the second beat of the measure, so count them "2 &".

Swedish Folk Song

• **2. Mark the tablature directly below each note with the correct fret number, or "o" for "open," on the correct string. Use arabic numerals.**

The double bars with dots are **repeat signs**.

When playing the piece, repeat from measure 4 to the beginning and play measures 1 – 4 a second time. Play to the end of the piece, then repeat *from measure 5*, which is the nearest *reverse* repeat sign.

Ode to Joy

From the Ninth Symphony   Ludwig van Beethoven

• **3. Mark the tablature directly below each note with the correct fret number, or "o" for "open," on the correct string. Use arabic numerals.**

This version of the "Ode to Joy" is written one octave lower than the previous version, p.28. It provides tablature and reading practice on the middle set of strings in first position. Notice how different the finger patterns are from the version played on the higher strings, even though the pitch classes are identical. This is one of the big differences between reading on the fretboard and on a keyboard, where the fingering and layout of black and white keys is identical for transpositions by the octave.

Aura Lea

Nineteenth Century American   George R. Poulton

• 4. Mark the tablature directly below each note with the correct fret number, or "o" for "open," on the correct string. Use arabic numerals.

"Aura Lea" provides reading and tablature practice on the lower strings in first position. You may recognize the melody, which was made famous as a popular song with a different title.

▶ **For an extra project, transpose "Aura Lea" an octave higher** by thinking the letter names on the higher strings. The first note "G" would begin on string ③ open. Use blank staff paper to notate this version. [Blank staff and tablature pages are included in the back of this book.]

❯ C. Converting Guitar Tablature to Music Notation.

Visualizing music staff notes when thinking fretboard locations is essential to reading fluently on the guitar. In previous exercises, notation was converted to tablature. By reversing this process and converting *tablature to notation,* you will experience visualizing the music staff from the fretboard. "Good King Wenceslas" and "Aunt Rhody," on the following page, provide practice writing notation for first position notes.

• *For both pieces, write the staff notes directly above each tab mark. All are quarter notes except those with small half- or whole-notes above. Be sure the pitch level ["register"] on the staff is correct, as discussed in Section A of this chapter.*

• *Write letter names above each note.*

Good King Wenceslas

English Carol

Aunt Rhody

American Folk Song

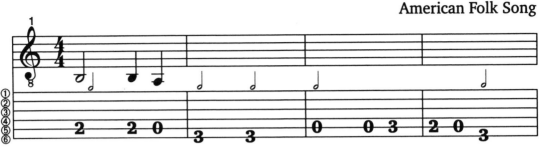

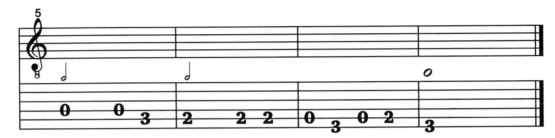

▶ D. Mixed Tablature and Notation: *Exercise*

The "Exercise" on the next two pages is from a method teaching classic guitar by Ferdinando Carulli, 1770 - 1841. It includes all the natural notes in first position. Write the tablature and notation, then play the piece.

The score includes both a music staff and six-line tablature underneath. Some lines ["systems"] show staff notation, and some show the tablature marks.

1. ***Where staff notation is given:*** Underneath each note, write the fret number on the string needed to play that note.

2. ***Where tablature marks are given:*** Above each string / fret mark, write the note on the music staff.

3. ***Letter name:*** Write the letter name above each note.

4. ***Suggestions and Reminders:***

   A. Note stems should go *up from the right side* for any note lower than the third [middle] line. Note stems should go *down from the left side* for any note on or higher than the third [middle] line.

   B. Remember to locate the "high," "middle," or "low" version for each letter correctly. The clef-sign "G," [string ③ open] is the landmark. If a note or tab mark is higher than this "G," it will be higher on the staff or tablature also. If a note or tab mark is lower than this "G," it will be lower on the staff or tablature also.

33

Exercise

Ferdinando Carulli, 1770–1841

▶ *Chapter 5*

Chord Basics

▶ A. Chord Diagrams for Guitar.

Chord diagrams are a visual pattern of the guitar strings and frets, with dots to show where left hand fingers are placed. The tablature presented in Chapter 4 showed the strings *horizontally* so the marks could relate to the left - right direction of reading from the music staff. Chord diagrams, however, show the strings *vertically*. This system is more convenient for chords, because they are fingered at a point in time, and do not change until the next different chord is shown.

The left hand fingers are placed *to the left of the fret* as close as possible, but *not* on top of the fret. This produces the clearest tone. The thumb is placed as a guide behind the neck, with pressure at the middle joint, *not* at the tip. Imagine the thumb parallel to the frets, opposite the second (middle) finger.

▶ B. Guidelines for Playing the Correct Chord Strings.

1. *A note, or pitch, is the tone produced by playing one string alone.*

Single notes (learned in Chapter 3) are designated by a *letter name only.* For example: "A," "C# (C-sharp)," "D," "Eb (E-flat)."

2. *A chord is the sound produced by playing three or more strings.*

By definition, a chord requires *three or more letters* played and blended together. On a music staff, a chord would have 3 or more different notes. *Only one letter*, however, lends the chord its name. Chords are identified by this letter name and frequently by additional qualities such as "m" ["minor"], "7," "dim" ["diminished"], "b5," ["flat 5], and others. A plain letter indicates a *major* triad [three-letter chord].

3. *The single note which gives the whole chord its letter name is termed the "root."*

The root is rather like an "initial" for the entire chord spelling. The other letters are "understood, " as learned from study of chord construction and the chord symbol system. Some examples:

- The root of the C chord is "C."
- The root of the Em chord is "E."
- The root of the Bb7 chord is "Bb."
- The root of the F#dim7 chord is "F#."

> **The lowest string for any chord**
> **should be the one which is**
> **the *root* of that chord.**

• *Not all strings are played for every chord. In selecting the lowest string for a chord, apply Guidelines A, B or C, in order:*

A. Use the open string which names the chord.

For example:

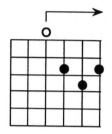

Chord: **D**

Root: **D**

Playing begins with the open "D" string ④ .
Only four strings are played.

B. Use the lowest string fretted by the left hand.

The root may be a note included in the chord fingering.

For example:

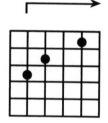

Chord: **C**

Root: **C**

Playing begins with the note "C" on string ⑤
Five strings are played.

C. Use the lowest open string included in the chord diagram, even if it is not the root.

Sometimes simplified fingerings are given for chords that might be difficult for less experienced players. They may show an "O" at a low open string which is not the root of the chord. It is all right to include this string, especially if only three strings would be included otherwise. *This guideline should always be a "last resort" after applying those described in "A" and "B" above.*

For example:

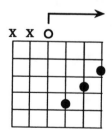

Chord: **Bm** ("B minor")

Root: **B**

The "O" indicates that string ④ open can be included in the chord. The "X's" are strings that *must not* be included. Playing four strings produces a bigger sound than playing just three strings, beginning with the fingered "B" on string ③.

38

◗ C. **Beginning Chord Fingering Exercises.**

The purpose of these exercises is to practice chord fingerings. Each exercise has chords with similar fretboard patterns. Tablatures are shown only the first time each chord occurs. Blank tablatures are included for repeated uses of chords. They may be used to draw in fingerings for a reminder and memory aid.

Left hand finger numbers are not shown for chords that can be fingered more than one way. It is important to place as many fingers as possible as close to the frets as possible. Where finger numbers are included, they are the best choices for the chord and should be the only ones used during the earlier stages of learning guitar.

> • *Finger and strum each chord in the order shown.*
> • *Be sure to start with the correct low "root string" for each chord.*

• *Fingerings at frets II and III.*

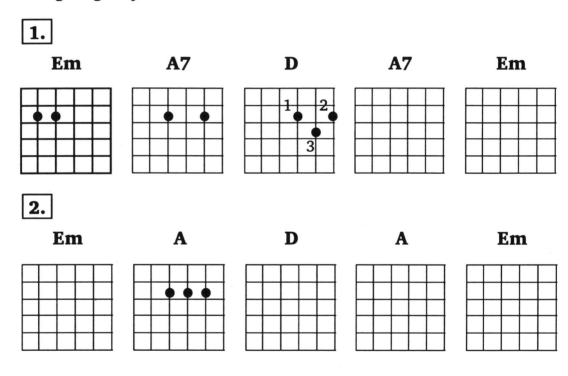

• *Fingerings at frets I and II [continued].*

4.

B7	E	Am	E	B7

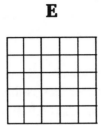 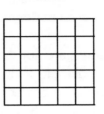 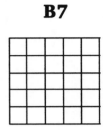

• *Similar fingering shapes: fingers 1 and 2.*

5.

E7	Am	Dm	Am	E7

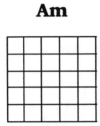 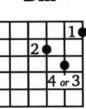 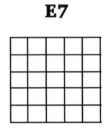

• *Fingerings at frets I, II and III.*

6.

G7	C	F	C	G7

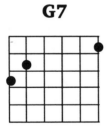 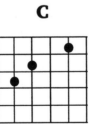 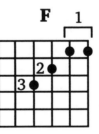 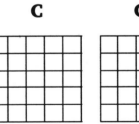 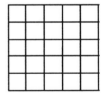

7.

C7	F	Dm	F	C7

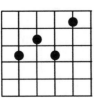 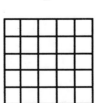 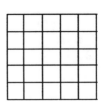 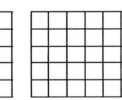

• *One or more finger positions common to consecutive chords.*
Fingers can be chosen for each chord so that one or more will stay at the same string and fret when changing to the next chord.

8.

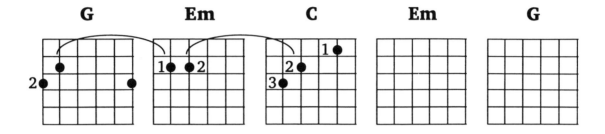

9.

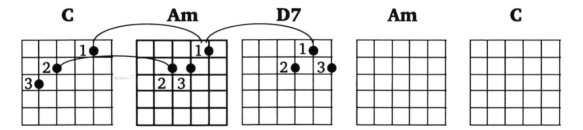

• *Draw in the finger dots and finger numbers in this chord series.*
• *Draw lines to show finger connections.*

10.

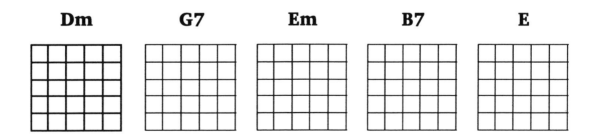

▶ *Chapter 6*
Song Accompaniment and Charts

▶ A. Songs with One Chord.

Each of these songs can be accompanied with just one chord. Several chords are suggested for each song. Strum *one* of them for the entire song. The first note for singing each song is the root of the chord played. *For example:* If the G chord is used to accompany "Frere Jacques," play the *single note* "G" to hear the first tone to sing.

Row, Row, Row Your Boat
Chord choices: A, C, D, E, G

Row, row, row your boat, gently down the stream.
Merrily, merrily, merrily, merrily, life is but a dream.

Frere Jacques
Chord choices: A, C, D, E, G

Frere Jacques, Frere Jacques, dormez vous?, dormez vous?
Sonnez les matines, sonnez les matines, Din, din, don; din, din, don.

Hey, Ho, Nobody Home
Chord choices: Am, Dm, Em

Hey, Ho, nobody home.
Meat nor drink nor money have I none.
Yet will I be merry.

▶ B. Song Accompaniment.

The melody for singing is notated on a music staff with chord names printed above.

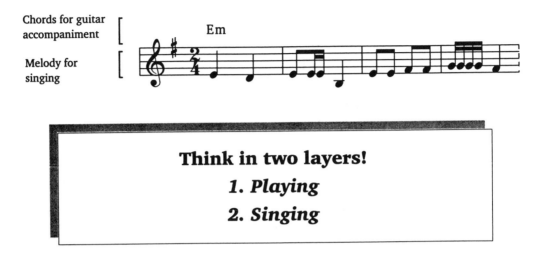

Think in two layers!
1. Playing
2. Singing

The guitar accompaniment blends with the singing line, but is not identical. It coordinates in two ways:

1. *Harmony.* The chord sounds blend with the melody, but are not identical.

2. *Rhythmic pulse.* The guitar plays at the same tempo (speed) as the singing. The pulse is determined by the number of beats per measure, and by the style of the song itself: slow, medium, or fast.

The diagonal beat marks in the following song show where the pulse and melody notes coincide. Notice that there are only two beats in each measure, even though some measures have more than two melody notes on the music staff.

Hey, Ho! Nobody Home

▶ C. Music Charts: The Three Basic Elements

Chords add harmony (depth of sound) and rhythm (movement) to the vocal line of a song. Three elements are required to play a chord accompaniment:

1. ***Time signature.*** This is the set of two numbers which appears at the beginning of a song or chart. The most common time signatures are 3/4, 4/4, 2/4 and 6/8.

   The top number is the essential one for chord accompaniments. It indicates the number of beats in one measure.

   The lower number indicates the kind of note that gets one beat. The number "4" represents a quarter note, and "8" an eighth note.

2. ***Measures.*** The "space" between barlines is a "measure."

3. ***Chord names.*** These are either above the music staff, or within the barlines in a chart. Only changes to new chords are written. The same chord is played and counted until a new one is shown.

**A chart shows *only* the
time signature,
measures and chord names.**

The above sample chart has four measures. The top number of the time signature indicates three beats in each measure. (Three beats multiplied by four measures means that there are a total of twelve beats in this brief example.)

- *The first chord, Em, is played for one measure (three beats).*
- *The second chord, Am, is then played for one measure (three beats).*
- *The third chord, Em, is played for two measures, counted "1 – 2 – 3 – 1 – 2 – 3."*

Each measure should be counted separately, so that the number "one" always means that the "next" measure is beginning.

▶ D. Chart Exercises.

- *Play these chart exercises to practice counting and chord changes.*
- *Strum once for each beat in the measure.*

For example: If there are four beats per measure, strum four times, counting "1 – 2 – 3 – 4." Then move on to the next measure. If it is "blank," continue strumming the same chord. If a different chord is named, change to the new fingering. Continue strumming and counting in the same way to the end of the exercise.

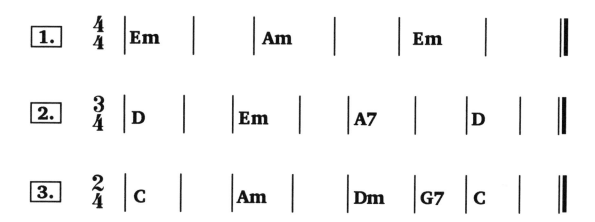

- *In the next two exercises, repeat from the repeat mark as many times as you wish.*
- *Play the final chord the last time only.*

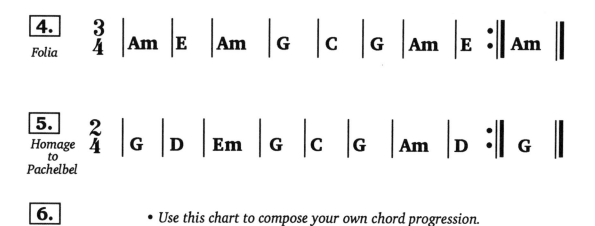

6. • *Use this chart to compose your own chord progression.*
• *Add the top number to the time signature and choose the chords.*

▶ *Chapter 7*

Songs: Charts with Words

▶ A. Charts with Words.

Familiar songs can be played from charts with the words added. Play the three songs "Skip to My Lou," "Amazing Grace," and "Scarborough Fair" by strumming once for each beat. Count beats per measure, as learned in the previous chapter. Sing along after the counting and chord changes become secure.

After studying rhythmic variety in Chapter 8, play these songs again using the special strum patterns shown here.

Skip to My Lou

Refrain

$\frac{2}{4}$

| **D** | | **A7** | |
| Skip, skip | skip to my Lou; | Skip, skip | skip to my Lou; |

| **D** | | **A7** | **D** |
| Skip, skip | skip to my Lou; | skip to my Lou my | darling. |

Verse

| **D** | |
| Flies in the buttermilk, | Shoo fly shoo. |

| **A7** | |
| Flies in the buttermilk, | Shoo fly shoo. |

| **D** | |
| Flies in the buttermilk, | Shoo fly shoo. |

| **A7** | **D** |
| skip to my Lou my | darling. |

Special strum rhythm:

Amazing Grace

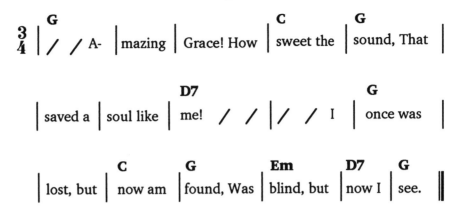

$\frac{3}{4}$ | / / A- | mazing | Grace! How | sweet the | sound, That |

| saved a | soul like | me! / / | / / I | once was |

| lost, but | now am | found, Was | blind, but | now I | see. ‖

2. 'Twas grace that taught my heart to fear,
   And grace my fears relieved;
   How precious did that grace appear
   The hour I first believed!

Special strum rhythm:

Scarborough Fair

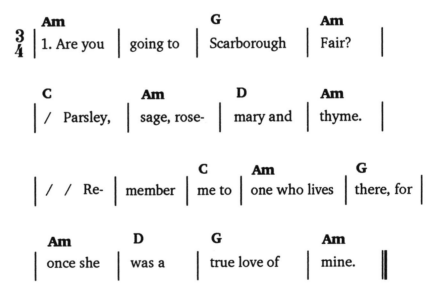

$\frac{3}{4}$ | 1. Are you | going to | Scarborough | Fair? |

| / Parsley, | sage, rose- | mary and | thyme. |

| / / Re- | member | me to | one who lives | there, for |

| once she | was a | true love of | mine. ‖

2. Have her make me a cambric shirt,
   Parsley, sage, rosemary and thyme.
   Without a seam or fine needle work,
   And then she'll be a true love of mine.

Special strum rhythm:

▶ B. Memorizing Chords Alphabetically.

The chords in this book are chosen for beginners because they are the ones most used in folk, country and gospel music. They are known as "open position" fingerings because they involve a mix of open and fingered strings, and are physically the easiest. Knowledge of these chords opens the door to learning a more comprehensive group of chords known as "moveable" or "bar" forms. They are derived from the fingerings of the open position chords.

This basic group of chords includes only three types: major ("plain letter" chords), minor, and "7th." These three categories are not complete for every root letter given here, however, because some would require fingerings that are physically difficult for many beginners on guitar.

Although chord fingerings are learned as they are used in songs over time, they can be memorized by thinking them through alphabetically. Apply the "major, minor, 7th" category to each letter, and skip over those not included in this book.

- *Use the blank tablatures on this page to draw fingerings for each chord.*
- *Write finger numbers beside each finger dot and use "o" to show open strings played.*
- *Use "x" to show strings not played.*
- *Use the letter "R" to mark the low root string for each chord.*
- *Play through the list without looking at this page to memorize fingerings.*

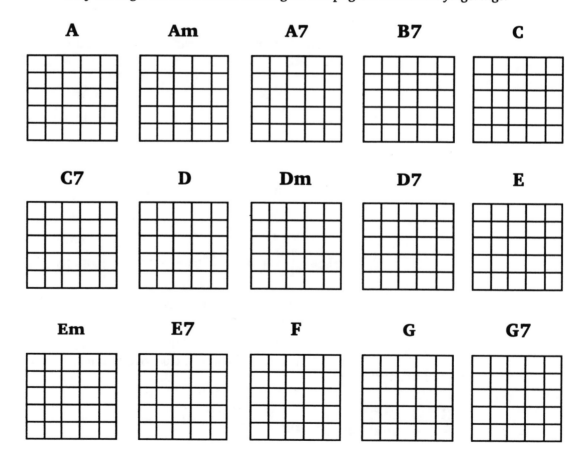

Chapter 8
Counting by Note Values

▶ A. Counting Values of Notes.

Chord accompaniments for songs can be played with rhythms other than simply strumming once for each beat. A wide variety is possible by using rhythmic notation to diagram strum rhythms. Different lengths of time are shown by different note values.

♩ *Quarter note: 1 beat.* Count "1" for each note.

♩ *Half note: 2 beats.* Count "1-2" for each note.

♩. *Dotted Half note: 3 beats.* Count "1-2-3" for each note.

○ *Whole note: 4 beats.* Count "1-2-3-4" for each note.

♫ *Eighth-notes: 1/2 beat each* Count "1 and " for the pair. Two 8th notes get one beat, and are equivalent to one quarter note.

▶ B. Counting Individual Note Values.

Counting each note for its own value is a first step in learning to read rhythm notation. Use the following exercises to practice this type of counting.

• *Finger the indicated chords and strum a down-stroke on each note.*

• *Say aloud **all** the numbers which apply to each note, as the examples show.*

• *Speak them at the same speed, as though your voice is a "clock."*
This will guarantee that each note lasts long enough.

• *Since each note is counted separately, strum only on the number "1."*

• *The counting numbers in the first measure provide a model for the whole exercise, but watch for changed rhythms near the end of some of the exercises.*

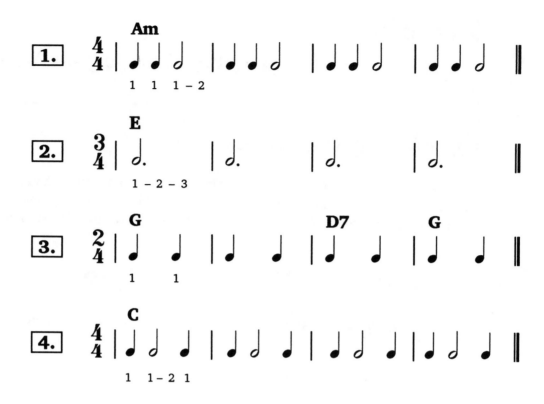

- Strum **down** on quarter, half, dotted-half, and whole notes.
- Always strum **down-up on eighth notes:** down on the first note and up on the "&."
- The arrows in #5 are a model for all the exercises.

▶ C. Counting Beats per Measure.

When a piece of music is counted, the beats for different note values are numbered according to their place in the measure.

• Strum and count Exercises #1 – 4.
• Use the counting numbers in the first measure as a model.

• Write the counting numbers for exercises #5 – 7, matching them to the correct beats.
• Play each exercise by strumming and counting aloud.

▶ *Chapter 9*
Converting Songs to Charts

▶ A. Published Song Formats and Conversion to Charts.

Songs are generally published in one of these two formats:

1. **Lead sheet.** This form has one music staff on which the melody is notated. Words are included, and chord names are above the staff. It is used frequently by bands, studio, and club musicians, and may be found in special guitar editions. It is a kind of "short-hand" of the music for improvising musicians, and is very practical because it conserves space and prevents page-turns.

> • *The songs in this book are in lead sheet format.*

2. *Piano – Vocal – Guitar score.* This is the common format of sheet music and song anthologies. It consists of three staves: a lead sheet for the vocal line, plus a two-stave grand staff with a keyboard arrangement of the song. The chords are above the vocal staff, and are useful for any of the instruments playing the music. The keyboard part may be played as published, or can be improvised from the chords and melody.

**When playing chord accompaniments,
reduce lead sheets to a basic chart:
1. Time signature   2. Measures   3. Chords**

He's Got the Whole World in His Hands

Traditional

He's got the   whole world———   in   His   hands   He's got the

whole world———   in   His   hands   He's got the   whole world———

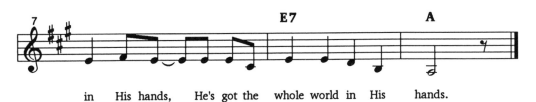

in   His   hands,   He's got the   whole world in   His   hands.

1. He's got the little bitty baby, *etc.*
2. He's got you and me, brother, *etc.*
3. He's got you and me, sister, *etc.*
4. He's got the wind and the rain, *etc.*

"*He's Got the Whole World in His Hands*" is written in lead sheet form.

When reduced to a basic chart, it looks like this:

$\frac{4}{4}$ **A** | | | **E7** | **A** | | **E7** | **A** ‖

• *Play the chart alone before singing the song.*

Playing techniques

1. Strum once for each beat.

2. Mixed rhythm strum.

When the Saints Go Marching In

• *Draw a chart of this song here.*

B.   Variety of Playing Techniques.

Mixed rhythms (Chapter 8) introduced one way to vary chord accompaniments. Three additional strumming methods will be described for the remaining songs in this chapter. The "brush-damp" stroke is described below. It is suitable for "When the Saints Go Marching In," and also for "He's Got the Whole World in His Hands." As you learn a variety of techniques, you can play different rhythms for different verses of the same songs.

Playing technique: "Brush-Damp" stroke.

Brush :   Make a light fist, then brush the fingernails across the strings with a flicking motion as you open your hand.

Damp :   Use the same movement as for a "brush," but finish with the palm resting on the strings, thus "damping off" the sound.

As with all accompaniment rhythms, the strokes must be coordinated with the beats of the measure.

Down in the Valley

Traditional

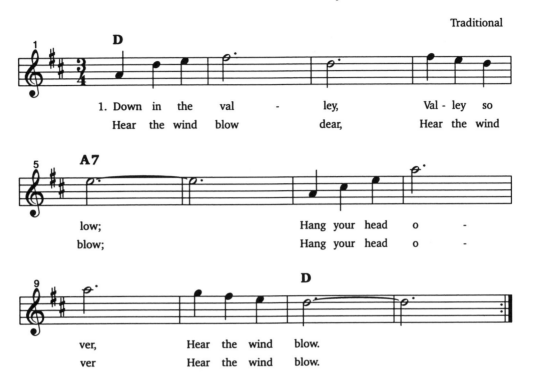

1. Down in the val - ley,   Val - ley so
Hear the wind blow   dear,   Hear the wind

low;   Hang your head   o   -
blow;   Hang your head   o   -

ver,   Hear the wind blow.
ver   Hear the wind blow.

2. Roses love sunshine, violets love dew.
   Angels in heaven, know I love you.
   Know I love you, dear, know I love you,
   Angels in heaven, know I love you.

• **Draw a chart of this song here.**

| Playing technique: "Root - Chord" stroke. |

Root :   Play the string for the root by itself, either with the pick or with the right hand thumb.

Chord :   Follow the root with the rest of the strings for the chord. Either strum with the pick, or use the "brush" stroke with the hand.

As with all accompaniment rhythms, the strokes must be coordinated with the beats of the measure.

Root Chord Chord

The Wabash Cannonball

American Traditional

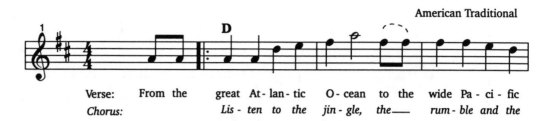

Verse: From the great At - lan - tic O - cean to the wide Pa - ci - fic
Chorus: Lis - ten to the jin - gle, the—— rum - ble and the

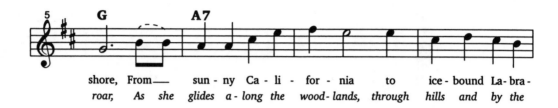

shore, From—— sun - ny Ca - li - for - nia to ice - bound La - bra -
roar, As she glides a - long the wood - lands, through hills and by the

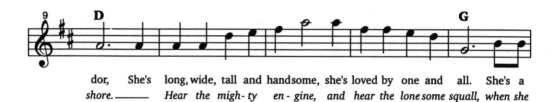

dor, She's long, wide, tall and handsome, she's loved by one and all. She's a
shore.—— Hear the migh - ty en - gine, and hear the lonesome squall, when she

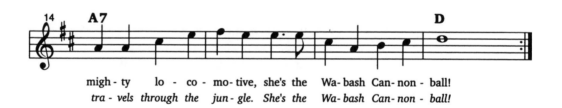

migh - ty lo - co - mo - tive, she's the Wa - bash Can - non - ball!
tra - vels through the jun - gle. She's the Wa - bash Can - non - ball!

• **Draw a chart of this song here.**

Playing techniques

1. Root - Chord.

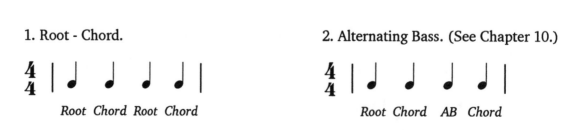

Root Chord Root Chord

2. Alternating Bass. (See Chapter 10.)

Root Chord AB Chord

▶ *Chapter 10*
Alternating Bass for Chords

▶ A. Definition of "Alternating Bass."

"Alternating bass" ["AB"] means simply that the root of the chord "alternates" with another chord tone in the bass part of the strumming or freestroke ("finger-picking") pattern. Alternating bass is used especially in folk and country music as a way of adding variety to the sound of a chord that lasts for some time. It can be used with any freestroke pattern and any strumming technique which includes single bass strings, rather than strumming whole chords in a single stroke.

The first choice for a bass string is the root of the chord. The root may be followed and alternated with a different note belonging to the same chord. For example, a "root-chord" strumming pattern with alternating bass in 4/4 meter would be played this way:

$$\frac{4}{4}$$ ♩ ♩ ♩ ♩

Root Chord AB Chord

▶ B. Perfect Fifths as Alternating Basses.

Music theory offers many helpful shortcuts to learning the guitar. One such shortcut is the system for figuring out alternating bass notes for different chords. It is possible to use any note, any string, belonging to a chord as an alternating bass. However, the one heard most frequently in bluegrass and folk music is the *fifth of the chord*. This is the letter an interval of a *fifth above the root*.

> **When counting intervals in music,**
> **the starting letter is number "1."**
> *Do not add, as in math!*

A B C D E

1 2 3 4 5

Using the above example, the language of music theory would say that

"B is an interval of a *second* higher than A."
"C is an interval of a *third* higher than A."
"D is an interval of a *fourth* higher than A."
"E is an interval of a *fifth* higher than A."

The example below relates the fifth interval, used for alternating basses, to chord roots:

Chord	*Root*	*Fifth*
A	A	E
C	C	G
C#	C#	G#

Chord roots and fifths are termed "perfect fifths," and, with only one exception, have matched accidentals.

If a root is sharp, the 5th is sharp.
If a root is flat, the 5th is flat.
If a root is natural, the 5th is natural.
The only exceptions are between "B" and "F."

When the root is B, the perfect fifth is F#.

When the root is Bb, the perfect fifth is F natural.

• *Study the examples and write in answers for the rest of this chart:*

Chord	Root	Fifth	Chord	Root	Fifth
B	B	F#	Cb	___	___
Db	Db	Ab	Eb	___	___
F	F	C	Gb	___	___
Ab	___	___	D	___	___
E	___	___	C	___	___
G	___	___	A	___	___
Bb	___	___	C#	___	___
F#	___	___			

▶ C. – But Not All Chords Have Perfect Fifths!

All three types of chords taught in this book, major, minor, and seventh, have the root – perfect fifth relationship described above. They are the ones for which alternating bass technique is used. However, the following types of chords differ as described:

1. **Diminished chords have a fifth that is lowered by a half-step chromatically.**

   The alphabet letter is the fifth higher than the root, but is a *half-step lower* than a perfect fifth. For example, if a root – perfect fifth is **C – G**, the *diminished fifth* would be **C – Gb.**

   Samples of diminished chord symbols are E°, Edim, and Em^{b5} .

2. **Flat-fifth chords have a fifth that is lowered by a half-step chromatically.**

   The rule is the same as for diminished chords, but the chord symbols are different.

   Samples of flat-fifth chord symbols are D^{b5}, D7$^{(b5)}$, and Dm7^{-5}.

3. *Augmented chords have a fifth that is raised by a half-step chromatically.*

The alphabet letter is also the fifth higher than the root, but is a *half-step higher* than a perfect fifth. For example, if a root – perfect fifth is **C – G**, the *augmented fifth* would be **C – G#**.

Samples of augmented chord symbols are C+, Caug, and C$^{\#5}$.

A detailed discussion of all the chord types used in contemporary music is beyond the scope of this book, but should be studied by serious students. Many books are available for this purpose, especially those teaching jazz theory.

▶ D. Alternating Bass Applied to Various Chords.

To play the alternating bass on the guitar, locate the lowest note with the letter name of the fifth of the chord. Several examples are shown here.

Chord	Root: String/Fret	Fifth: String/Fret	Diagram	Technique
A [Am] [A7]	**A:** ⑤ open	**E:** ⑥ open		
B7	**B:** ⑤ II	**F#:** ⑥ II		
C [C7]	**C:** ⑤ III	**G:** ⑥ III		

Notice that the root is fingered in the chord form, but the 2nd finger must jump to the sixth string for the alternate bass.

The root is fingered in the chord form, but the 3d finger must jump to the sixth string for the alternate bass.

60

- *Write in the information for the following chords using the preceding chart as a model.*
  - *Diagram only the major chord.*

Chord	Root: String/Fret	Fifth: String/Fret	Diagram	Technique
D **[Dm]** **[D7]**	_____	_____		
E **[Em]** **[E7]**	_____	_____		
F	_____	_____		
G **[G7]**	_____	_____		

▶ *Chapter 11*

Freestroke with Chords

▶ A. Freestroke Technique.

Freestroke is a standard technique in classic guitar music, and is frequently used in folk, country, bluegrass, and jazz styles. Also known as "finger-picking" or "fingerstyle," freestroke uses a plucking motion, with each finger on a separate string. The brushing action of strumming generally requires playing several *adjacent* strings together. The freestroke, however, makes it possible to skip strings, play several combined or one at a time, and to vary the order in which they are played. Thus the door is open to designing many more varied chord accompaniments.

Standard freestroke technique uses the thumb, index, middle and ring fingers of the right hand. Traditionally they are represented by the initials of the Spanish words for each finger:

   P: *pulgar* The **thumb** plays the bass (root or special letter).

   i: *indice* The **index** finger plays string ③.

   m: *medio* The **middle** finger plays string ②.

   a: *anular* The **ring** finger plays string ①.

The placement of fingers is shown in this tablature. Notice that because only four fingers are used, two of the six strings are not played.

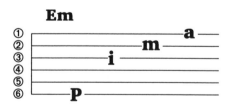

• The thumb changes to the low string needed for each chord root or special bass.

• The **i, m, a** fingers continue to play only the higher three strings for all chords.

62

> # The order and rhythm
> # of finger strokes combined produce a
> # *freestroke pattern.*

▶ B. Freestroke Patterns.

Finger strokes may be represented as rhythmic note values, just as strumming rhythms are. They are frequently in eighth-notes, meaning that two strokes are played for each beat in 2/4, 3/4, or 4/4 meter. Mixed note values are also possible, and must coordinate with the meter of the piece.

The following page has a chart of commonly used freestroke patterns as played with an E minor chord. They are just a few of the nearly infinite number of patterns available by varying note values and the order of finger strokes. When the fingerings are applied to other chords, the thumb plays the new root or special bass, but the **i m a** fingers remain on strings ①, ②, and ③.

▶ C. Beginning Steps for Playing a Freestroke Pattern.

• *Use these steps to play the patterns on the chart, as well as the songs in this chapter.*

1. Finger the chord with the left hand.

2. Place each of the right hand fingers on the correct string:

P: on the root or special bass string.
i: on string ③
m: on string ②
a: on string ①

[In advanced playing it is better *not* to rest the right hand fingers on the strings before playing.]

3. Play the fingers in the order and combination shown in the pattern, counting the rhythm correctly.

4. Play the song without singing until the freestroke becomes almost automatic. Then singing along will be much easier.

Freestroke Pattern Chart

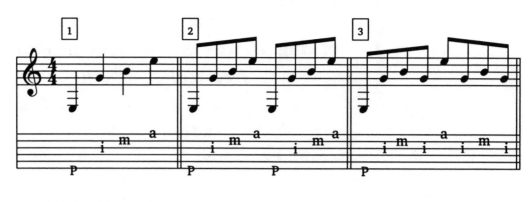

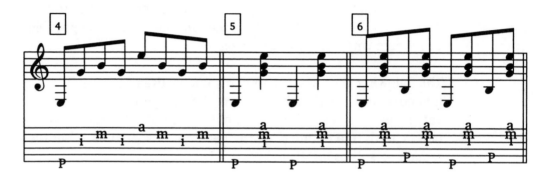

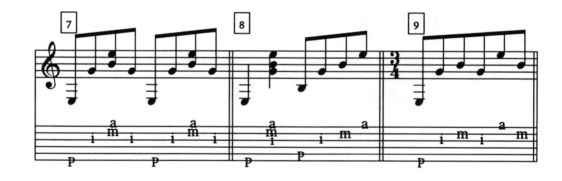

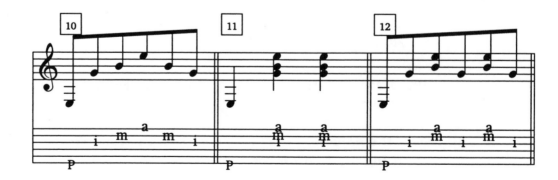

Riddle Song

Traditional American

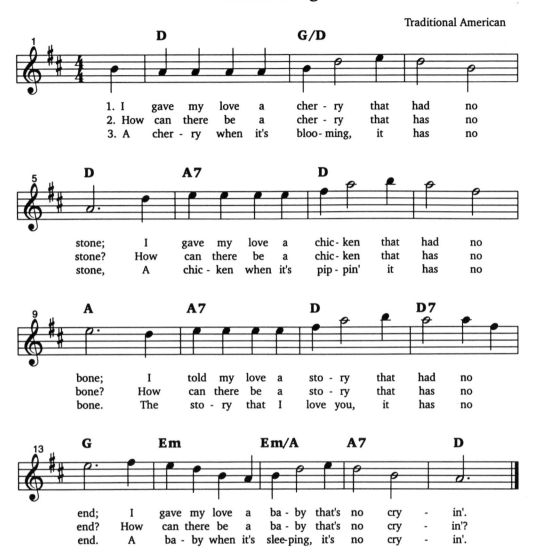

Special chord fingerings:

When chords have double letters separated by a slash, the true chord is the symbol to the left. The letter following the slash is a special note which *replaces the root* as the bass. Sometimes the chord fingering must be changed to provide this special bass, as in the Em/A chord. The chords required for the "Riddle Song" are shown below. [The "x's" mark strings that should *not* be played.]

Freestroke pattern:

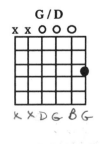

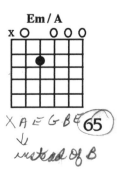

I. *Greensleeves*
II. *What Child is This?*

– 16th Century English
– William C. Dix, 1837-1898

I: A - las my love,— you do me wrong— to
II: What child is this— who laid to rest— on

cast me off— dis - cour - teous - ly. And I haved
Ma - ry's lap— is slee - ping? Whom an - gels

loved— you oh, so long— De - light - ing in— your
greet— with an - thems sweet,— While shep - herds watch— are

com - pa - ny. Green - sleeves— was all my joy,—
keep - ing? This, this— is Christ the King, Whom

Green - sleeves— was my de - light. Green - sleeves was my
shep - herds guard— and an - gels sing; Haste, haste— to

heart of gold,— And who but my la - dy Green - sleeves.
bring Him laud,— The Babe,— the Son— of Ma - ry.

Freestroke pattern:

String: Ⓡ ③ ② ① ② ③

66

Scarborough Fair

English Folk Song

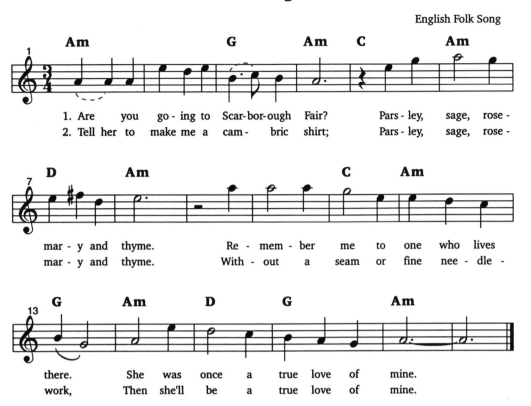

1. Are you go - ing to Scar-bor-ough Fair? Pars - ley, sage, rose -
2. Tell her to make me a cam - bric shirt; Pars - ley, sage, rose -

mar - y and thyme. Re - mem - ber me to one who lives
mar - y and thyme. With - out a seam or fine nee - dle -

there. She was once a true love of mine.
work, Then she'll be a true love of mine.

Draw a chart of this song here:

Freestroke pattern:

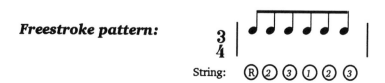

All Through the Night

Welsh Folk Song

Sleep my child and peace at-tend thee, All through the night.
Guar-dian an-gels God will send thee, All through the night.

Soft the drow-sy hours are creep-ing, hill and vale in slum-ber steep-ing;

I my lo-ving vig-il keep-ing, All through the night.

Draw a chart of this song here:

Special chord fingerings:

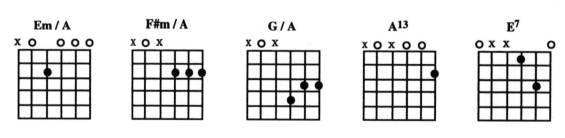

Freestroke pattern:

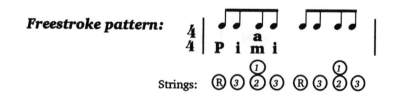

Aura Lea

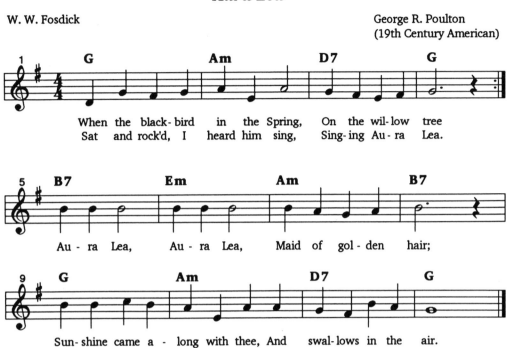

W. W. Fosdick

George R. Poulton
(19th Century American)

When the black-bird in the Spring, On the wil-low tree
Sat and rock'd, I heard him sing, Sing-ing Au-ra Lea.

Au - ra Lea, Au - ra Lea, Maid of gol-den hair;

Sun-shine came a - long with thee, And swal-lows in the air.

Draw a chart of this song here:

Freestroke pattern:

▶ *Chapter 12*

The Chords Most Likely to Succeed

▶ A. Practice Chart for Primary Key Chords.

A key is a musical environment in which a specific formula of whole- and half-steps determines the alphabetical list of notes. This list, or scale, is the source of chord and melody notes for the key. The scale formula determines whether a key is major, minor, or modal.

The chart below lists the three most important chords for keys often found in guitar song playing. These three chords are the "primary" chords. They are especially useful because *all scale notes for the key* occur someplace in one of these three chords. Six of the seven different scale tones are present in just two chords, the I and V7. This means that all the notes of a scale, or melody using that scale, might be harmonized with these three chords alone.

Learning the three primary chords for each key as a group is excellent preparation for "playing by ear." This chart does not list all possible keys, but includes those that can be played with the basic chords of beginning guitar.

* *Play the chords in order, left to right, as shown.*

* *For practice, they may be played with any strum or freestroke technique.*

Key	I Tonic	IV Subdominant	V7 Dominant	I Tonic
A major	A	D	E7	A
C major	C	F	G7	C
D major	D	G	A7	D
E major	E	A	B7	E
G major	G	C	D7	G
A minor	Am	Dm	E7	Am
E minor	Em	Am	B7	Em

▶ B. "The Chords Most Likely to Succeed."

In the traditional harmony associated with most folk, country and gospel music, the primary chords of the selected key are "most likely to succeed" in harmonizing a melody. These chords are useful for accompanying a familiar tune "by ear" when a written version is not available. They can also be used by songwriters as a starting point for harmonizing new tunes.

1. *In major keys, all three primary chords are major chords.*

The dominant chord may be used as a simple major triad, but quite frequently occurs as a 7th chord. [The "7" indicates that the seventh scale letter higher than the chord root has been added to the basic three-note chord, or "triad."]

2. *In minor keys, the tonic and subdominant chords are minor.*
The dominant-seventh is the same as for major.

The three forms of the minor scale provide more variety of chord types, but this formula is a useful starting point. It is also possible for the subdominant chord to be major, and the dominant chord minor, but *the tonic of a minor key is always minor.*

3. *The roots of primary chords are numbered by their place in the scale.*

The root of the tonic chord (I) is the *first* note of the scale.
The root of the subdominant chord (IV) is the *fourth* note of the scale.
The root of the dominant chord (V) is the *fifth* note of the scale.

4. *The roots of primary chords are all perfect fourths or fifths apart.*

Therefore they have matched accidentals, with the exception of the notes B – F.
• If the root of I is sharp, the roots of IV and V7 are also sharp.
• If the root of I is flat, the roots of IV and V7 are also flat.
• If the root of I is natural, the roots of IV and V are also natural.

The only exceptions to matched roots of primary chords are keys involving B or F as the tonic, as shown here. (Unmatched roots are in bold italics.)

Key	I	IV	V
Bb	*Bb*	Eb	*F*
B	*B*	E	*F#*
F	*F*	*Bb*	C
F#	*F#*	*B*	C#

• *Memorize the I – IV – V7 root relationships for the primary chords.*

• *Study the examples on this chart, then write in the remaining answers. Only keys involving the chords required in this book are included here.*

Key	I	IV	V7
A	A	D	E7
C	C	F	G7
D	__	__	__
E	__	__	__
G	__	__	__
Am	__	__	__
Em	__	__	__

▶ C.   Guitar Techniques for Harmonizing "by ear."

1. Sing the tune in a comfortable range for your voice.

Be sure to try the entire melody because it may go exceptionally high or low at some point in the song.

2. Choose the first chord.

Try various major or minor chords to find one as close as possible to the comfortable voice range. Major keys are more common than minor keys, and with practice your ear will detect the difference.

3. Name the chosen key.

The chord chosen to start the song will name the key, and is therefore the tonic (I) chord. Rarely a song may begin with a chord other than the tonic, but this is very much the exception. The chord which fits *at the end of the song* is the tonic, if the first and last chords are different.

The tonic chord begins and ends a song.

It names the key.

4. *Determine the IV and V7 chords in the key of the chord chosen as I.*

Sing from the beginning of the song with the tonic chord. Where a chord change seems needed, try either one of the other chords in a "trial and error" process to find which fits best. There is no set order for these chords. Each individual song will vary. Sometimes there may be more than one possibility for the order of chords. Simply do the best you can. Occasionally a song requires only two chords. They are usually I and V7.

5. *Rhythm will have either a duple or triple pulse.*

• If the beat is *duple* ("**strong** weak **strong** weak"), plan a strum or freestroke in 2/4 or 4/4 meter.

• If the beat is *triple* ("**strong** weak weak"), plan a strum or freestroke in 3/4 meter.

▶ D. Songs to Harmonize: Two Chords.

• *Choose familiar songs to harmonize.*

• *Write in the chords for the key which is best for your voice.*

• *Chords for additional keys may be written in a different color for each key.*

• *The songs with two chords use I and V7.*

Mary Had a Little Lamb

$\frac{2}{4}$ | Mary had a | little lamb, | Little lamb, | little lamb. |

| Mary had a | little lamb, its | Fleece was white as | snow. ‖

London Bridge

2/4 | London Bridge is | falling down, | falling down, | falling down. |

| London Bridge is | falling down. | My fair | lady. |

| Take the key and | lock her up, | lock her up, | lock her up. |

| Take the key and | lock her up. | My fair | lady. ‖

• *The song "Alouette" will require some chord changes within the same measure. Where this is necessary, use diagonal beat marks [/] to show the number of beats for each chord.*

Alouette

4/4 | Alouette, | gentille Alou – ette, | Alouette, | je te plume – rai. ‖
Fine

| Je te plumerai la tête, | Je te plume – rai la tête, |

‖: Et la tête, Et la tête; :‖ Alouette, Alouette. | Oh! – ‖

Repeat as needed for additional verses.   *D. C. al Fine*

Additional verses:
Repeat all in reverse order at measure with repeat marks.

Je te plumerai le cou, –
Je te plumerai les ailes, –
Je te plumerai les pattes, –
Je te plumerai le dos, –
Je te plumerai la queue, –

▶ E. Songs to Harmonize: Three Chords.

Auld Lang Syne

$\frac{4}{4}$ | / / / Should | old acquaintance | be forgot, And | never brought to |

| mind? Should | old acquaintance | be forgot, And | days of auld lang |

| syne? For | auld lang | syne, my dear, For | auld lang | syne; We'll |

| take a cup of | kindness yet, For | auld lang | syne. ‖

Happy Birthday

$\frac{3}{4}$ | / / Happy | Birthday to | you, Happy | Birthday to | you, Happy |

| Birthday dear | friend! Happy | Birthday to | you! ‖

Twinkle, Twinkle Little Star

$\frac{4}{4}$ | Twinkle, twinkle, | little star. | How I wonder | what you are. |

| Up above the | world so high, | Like a diamond | in the sky. |

| Twinkle, twinkle, | little star. | How I wonder | what you are. ‖

He's a Jolly Good Fellow

$\frac{3}{4}$ | / / For | he's a | jolly good | fel – | low, For | he's a | jolly good |

| fel – | low, For | he's a | jolly good | fel – | low, Which | nobody |

| can de– | ny | / / Which | nobody | can de– | ny | / / Which |

| nobody | can de– | ny | / / For | he's a | jolly good | fel – |

| low, For | he's a | jolly good | fel – | low, For | he's a | jolly good |

| fel – | low, Which | nobody | can de– | ny! ‖

Silent Night

$\frac{3}{4}$ | Silent | night, | holy | night. | All is | calm, | All is | bright, |

| Round yon | virgin | Mother and | Child. |

| Holy | Infant so | tender and | mild. |

| Sleep in | heavenly | peace – | – – – | Sleep in | heavenly | peace. ‖

Dm 6⁷ C   G

p. 21

shelia w/ 1st finger

```
1  1  1  21  2  2  2
0  3  1  3  0  1  0  3
```

Reference A: Tuning the Guitar

Electronic tuners are affordable and very helpful to many beginners on the guitar. They are especially valuable for new strings, which need frequent adjustment. It is also important to learn to tune the guitar to itself and to train the ear to hear the relationships between the strings. This reference describes two common processes.

▶A. Matching Unison Pitches at the Fifth Fret.

1. Tune the sixth string.

The preferred method is use of the "A – 440" tuning fork, described in section B below. As an alternative, the sixth string may be tuned to the piano key "E" which is the *second* "E" to the left of middle C. When unable to get this pitch from a piano or another musician, it is best to leave the sixth string as it is, assuming the guitar is played and tuned regularly. Because of its thicker gauge and greater stability, the sixth string is least likely to go badly out of tune.

2. Tune the remaining strings.

On all strings except ③, the letter at the fifth fret is the *same one, at the same pitch, as the next higher open string.* For example, fret V (5) on string ⑥ is "A," the same letter as string ⑤ open. Therefore the guitar can be tuned to itself by matching each open string to fret V on the next lower sounding / higher-numbered string. The single exception is that fret IV (4) on string ③ must be used for the "B" of string ② open. Use this chart as a reference.

	Hold down: [String/fret]		*To hear the sound of:* [Open string]
1.	⑥	V	⑤
2.	⑤	V	④
3.	④	V	③
4.	③	IV	②
5.	②	V	①

▶ B. Use of the "A – 440" Tuning Fork.

1. *Match the harmonic* at fret V of string ⑤ to the tuning fork.*
   [See the definition of "harmonic" in the section below, "Tuning with Harmonics."]

2. *Match fret V of string ⑥ to open string ⑤.*

3. *Follow steps #2 - 5 on the previous page to finish tuning the guitar.*

"A – 440" is the international standard of musical pitch, which is related to the frequency of sound waves. The "440" represents "440 cycles per second."

▶ C. Tuning with Harmonics.

* Harmonics are produced by touching the string *over the fret* without holding the string down on the fretboard. Playing the string causes a clear, bell-like tone.

Harmonics may be used to tune the guitar in several ways. This is one common method.

String/fret...		is matched to:	
⑤ V	harmonic	A – 440 tuning fork	
⑥ V	harmonic	⑤ VII	harmonic
④ VII	harmonic	⑤ V	harmonic
③ VII	harmonic	④ V	harmonic
②	open	⑥ VII	harmonic
①	open	⑥ V	harmonic

▶ D. Tuning Tips.

Learning to identify precisely what you are hearing when tuning the guitar takes time and practice. Some of the following tips may prove useful.

1. Never change the string being fingered at the fifth fret. It is already tuned.

2. When two out-of-tune (different) pitches become tuned (the same), the sensation of vibrations changes from one of throbbing or pulsating to a level, steady quality.

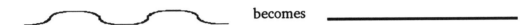   becomes

3. Sing from the string fingered at fret V to the open string being tuned.

    • If your voice changes *higher* to sing the open string, it is *too high (too tight)*. ***Loosen it to lower the pitch.***

    • If your voice changes *lower* to sing the open string, it is *too low (too loose)*. ***Tighten it to raise the pitch.***

    • If the pitches are very similar but pulsating or throbbing, the open string is *not* in tune. Use a best guess to judge whether it is too high or too low and change the string accordingly.

4. If you don't know whether a string is higher or lower, guess. (You have a 50% chance of being correct!) Tighten or loosen the string. If it gets further from the sound you want, change direction with the tuning peg. Listen for the two sounds to "melt" into one.

5. Always check tuning after any process (fifth fret, harmonics, or any others) is completed.

    • Play the two "E" strings. The sixth is lower sounding and the first higher, but they blend together very closely when in tune because both are the same letter name. (The frequency of the higher is an exact multiple of the frequency of the lower, thus causing considerable reinforcement of the wave forms and resulting tones.)

    • Play a variety of chords to hear whether all blend well. If a chord sounds poor, try playing the single strings of the chord to determine which one may be "off." Make the smallest adjustment possible to blend the chord, so other chords will not be drastically affected and thrown out of tune.

6. Be careful to relate to the "singing" sound of the strings. Different strings on the same guitar have a more or less difference in timbre, the quality or color element of sound. For example, timbre causes us to hear a flute as a different instrument from a violin, even when they are playing the same note.

    • The difference in timbre is due to the varying thicknesses of the strings. Different timbre also results from comparing strings which have a wound covering with those which are plain steel or nylon. Beginning guitarists are especially sensitive to this quality, so try to distinguish it from the "singing" pitch. ***Remember! It is the "singing" tone that must be matched!***

Reference B: Suggestions for Care and Maintenance

These suggestions are especially important for acoustic guitars, both steel-string and classic.

1. *Keep the guitar clean.*

Clean the body with guitar polish, available from music stores.

Normally the fretboard should *not* be polished, but it may need occasional rubbing with linseed oil, especially if it is a classic guitar. Ask a reputable guitar repair person or luthier if you are unsure what your guitar needs.

After playing, wipe strings, neck, and body with a dry soft cloth to remove oils and perspiration which can affect the finish.

2. *Keep the guitar in its case, away from dry, blowing hot air.*

Don't store it near hot air registers in winter, or in excessively hot spaces in summer. Wood is a natural, organic substance which reacts to sudden and extreme changes of temperature and humidity. The softer woods of the top and the harder woods of the back and sides of acoustic guitars expand and contract at different rates. Therefore excessive drying from lack of humidity and extreme, sudden changes of temperature stress the guitar. This may result in cracks, buckled wood, or other damage which is difficult or impossible to fix.

Do *not* leave a guitar in a car in freezing winter temperatures or summer sun.

Ideally the guitar should lie flat to prevent stress on the curved wood surfaces.

3. *Change strings regularly, and keep the guitar tuned to correct pitch.*

Change strings a minimum of twice a year, if not more often. New strings not only improve the sound, but provide the tension which helps to keep the neck in proper alignment. This is particularly important for classic guitars, which do not have a support rod in the neck for alignment adjustments.

Regular tuning to A–440 [as described in the "Tuning Reference" of this book] assures the correct amount of tension, and prevents excessive re-tuning problems.

When traveling with your guitar, especially by air, loosen the strings as a precaution against jarring which might damage the neck. [Consult your air carrier regarding their carry-on policy for guitars. If it must go in baggage, be sure it is in a locked hard case with strings loosened.]

NEVER put steel strings on a guitar made for nylon. It does not have a rod in the neck, and the much greater tension of steel can warp the neck beyond repair. When changing strings, do it correctly. Nylon strings wind from front to back over the barrel. Steel strings wind from the inside of the machine head toward the outside. Get help if you need it.

4. *If repairs or adjustments are needed, take your guitar to a reputable shop or luthier. Don't do it yourself.*

DISCLAIMER: *These are suggestions only.* Conditions and individual treatment of instruments vary sufficiently that this author cannot and does not assume any legal responsibility for the life and health of any guitar. It is solely the responsibility of the owner. Ask a local professional person for further advice.

Reference C: Answers

▶ Chapter 2

Page 8:

	Fret Number	Fret Half-step Higher	Fret Half-step Lower
A.	II (2)	III (3)	I (1)
B.	VII (7)	VIII (8)	VI (6)
C.	IV (4)	V (5)	III (3)
D.	Open string	I (1)	not possible on same string
E.	I (1)	II (2)	open string

Page 9:

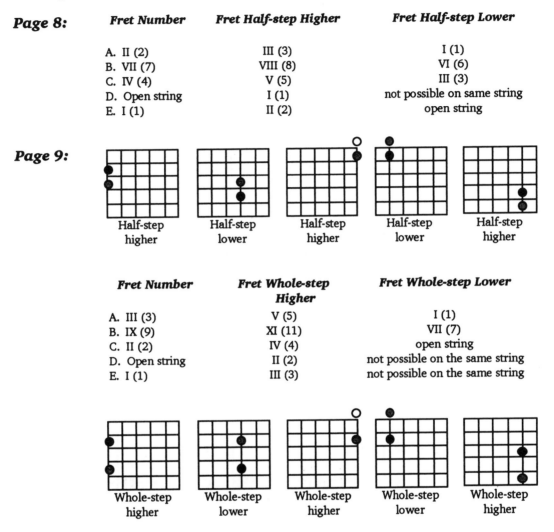

	Fret Number	Fret Whole-step Higher	Fret Whole-step Lower
A.	III (3)	V (5)	I (1)
B.	IX (9)	XI (11)	VII (7)
C.	II (2)	IV (4)	open string
D.	Open string	II (2)	not possible on the same string
E.	I (1)	III (3)	not possible on the same string

Page 10: Most natural notes are **2** [number] fret(s) apart, except B to C and E to F, which are **1** [number] fret(s) apart.

Page 11: Mark the appropriate answers: (Item "a" is marked as an example.)

	Letters	Half-step	Whole-step	One fret	Two frets
a.	**F – G**		✓		✓
b.	**C – D**		✓		✓
c.	**B – C**	✓		✓	
d.	**D – E**		✓		✓
e.	**A – B**		✓		✓
f.	**E – F**	✓		✓	
g.	**G – A**		✓		✓

Page 11:
Continued

1. Whole-step higher:

Letter name:

B

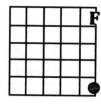

A (Open)

2. Whole-step lower:

Letter name:

F

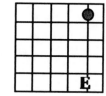

G

3. Two whole-steps higher:

Letter name:

A

F

4. Two whole-steps lower:

Letter name:

C

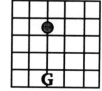

E

5. One whole and one half-step higher:

Letter name:

C

A

6. One whole and one half-step lower:

Letter name:

E

G

Page 12:

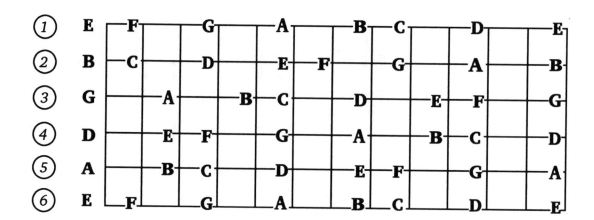

1. What is the number of the fret that has the same letter names as the open strings?
   Fret number **XII [12]**

2. Very few frets have letters [natural notes] across all six strings. Which frets are they?
   V, X, XII [5, 10, 12]

3. Which frets have letters on all but one string? **III, VII [3, 7]**

4. Only one fret has *no* natural letters on any string. Which fret? **XI [11]**

5. Which frets have only *one* letter on any of the strings? **IV, VI [4, 6]**

82

Page 13:

E F̲ G̲ A B̲ C̲ D E̲ F̲ G A̲ B̲ C̲ D̲ E F̲ G̲

Page 14:

Fretted tones: **F G / B C / E F / A / C D / F G**

Whole- or Half-steps: [H W] / W H / W H / W / H W / H W

Fret Numbers: [O I III] / O II III / O II III / O II / O I III / O I III

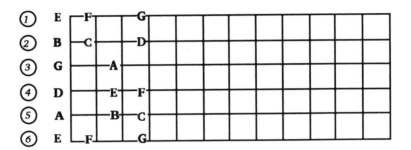

▌Chapter 3

Page 15:   [G A B] C D E F G

Page 16:   (Top of page): [G F E] D C B A G F E D C B A G F E

(Bottom of page): [E F] G A B C D E F G A B C D E F G

Page 17:   How many times does the letter "G" occur in this scale? _3_ .

The *low* G is on string number _6_ , fret number _III [3]_

The *middle* G is on string number _3_ , fret number _open_ .

The *high* G is on string number _1_ , fret number _III [3]_

▌Chapter 4

Use this "First Position Notation and Tablature Reference" to check your answers for the exercises in Chapter 4.

First Position Notation and Tablature Reference

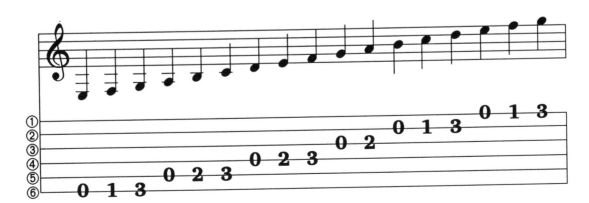

▶ **Chapter 5**   *Page 41:*

No. 10:   Fingers connecting the chords are:
        Dm to G7, finger 1   G7 to Em, finger 2   Em to B7, finger 2   B7 to E, finger 2

▶ **Chapter 8**   *Page 51:*

▶ **Chapter 9**   [Answers to charts for the songs on pages 54, 55, and 56 not given]

▶ **Chapter 10**
Page 59:

Chord	Root	Fifth
Ab	Ab	Eb
E	E	B
G	G	D
Bb	Bb	F
F#	F#	C#

Chord	Root	Fifth
Cb	Cb	Gb
Eb	Eb	Bb
Gb	Gb	Db
D	D	A
C	C	G
A	A	E
C#	C#	G#

Page 61:   [Answers not given]

▶ **Chapter 11**   [Answers to charts for the songs on pages 67, 68, and 69 not given]

▶ **Chapter 12**   *Page 72:*

Key	I	IV	V7
D	D	G	A7
E	E	A	B7
G	G	C	D7
Am	Am	Dm	E7
Em	Em	Am	B7

▶ Chapter 12, § D & E, Songs to Harmonize

Sample solutions are given here for three songs. If these keys are too high or too low for you to sing, you may transpose to other keys by changing the chords. Match the Roman numerals to the coordinating chords for each key, as shown in the chart on p. 70.

Mary Had a Little Lamb

2/4
| **D** [I] | | **A7** [V7] | **D** [I] | |
| Mary had a | little lamb, | Little lamb, | little lamb. | |

| | **A7** [V7] | **D** [I] | |
| Mary had a | little lamb, its | Fleece was white as | snow. ‖ |

Happy Birthday

3/4
| **G** [I] | | **D7** [V7] | **G** [I] | |
| / / Happy | Birthday to | you, Happy | Birthday to | you, Happy |

| | **C** [IV] | **G** [I] / **D7** **G** [I] | |
| Birthday dear | friend! Happy | Birthday to | you! ‖ |

Silent Night

3/4
| **A** [I] | | | | **E7** [V7] | | **A** [I] | | |
| Silent | night, | holy | night. | All is | calm, | All is | bright, | |

| **D** [IV] | | **A** [I] | | |
| Round yon | virgin | Mother and | Child. | |

| **D** [IV] | | **A** [I] | | |
| Holy | Infant so | tender and | mild. | |

| **E7** [V7] | | **A** [I] | | | | **E7** [V7] | **A** [I] | |
| Sleep in | heavenly | peace – | – – – | Sleep in | heavenly | peace. ‖ |

Reference D: Chords

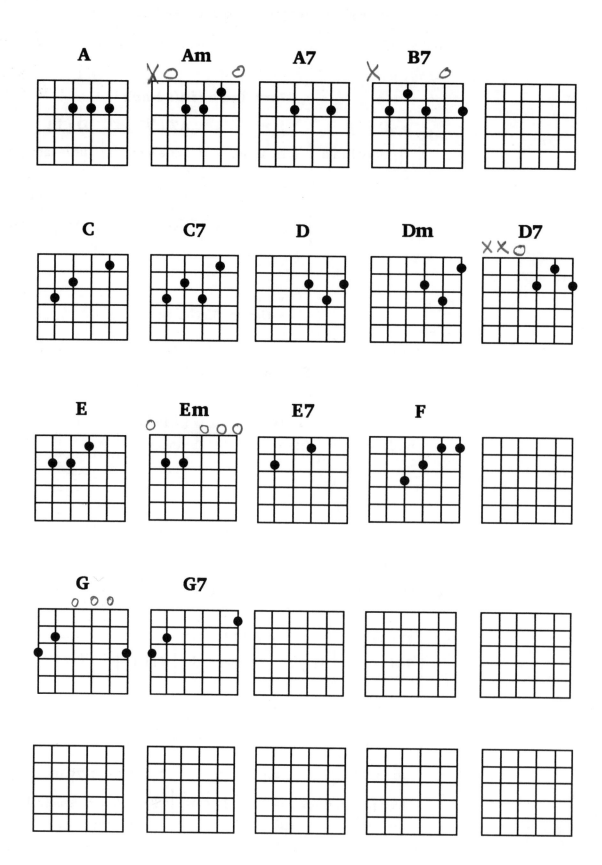

Blank Chord Diagrams

2/17 p. 65

C maj Scale Fingers

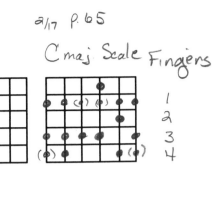

1
2
3
4

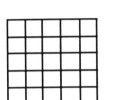 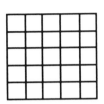 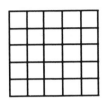 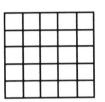 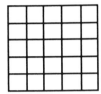

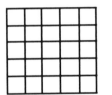 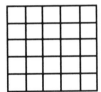 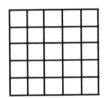 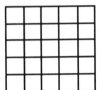 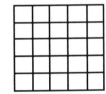

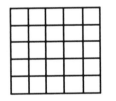 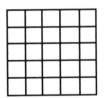 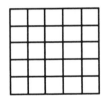 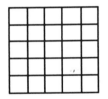 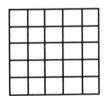

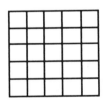 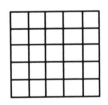 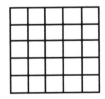 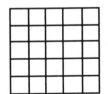 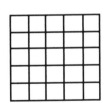

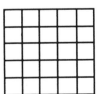 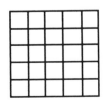 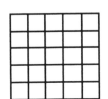 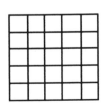 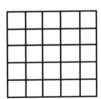

Blank Tablatures: 12 Frets

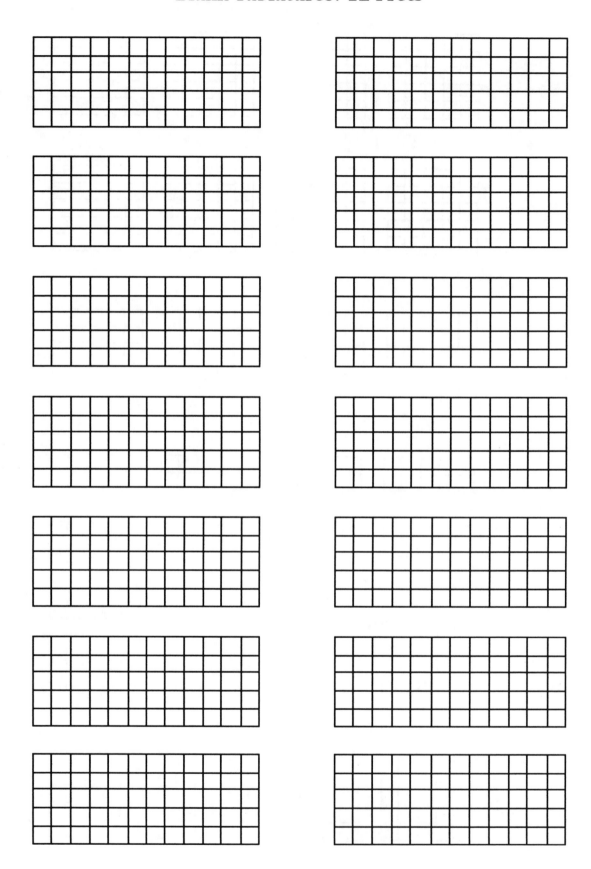

Practice Tablatures: Music Staff with Tab

Music Index